062 796

First Church of the Nazarene
3167 S. 10th St., Independence, KS 67301

From the Ends of the Earth

2012-13 NMI MISSION EDUCATION RESOURCES

✽ ✽ ✽

BOOKS

ADSIDEO
Cross-Cultural Ministry in the United States
By Bruce Nuffer

AFRICAN VOICES II
by Mark and Nancy Pitts

THE BEST OF ENGAGE MAGAZINE
Compelling and Inspiring Stories from the Mission Field
by Gina Grate Pottenger

FROM THE ENDS OF THE EARTH
The Growing Movement of Missionaries
from Non-Western Cultures
by Ellen Decker

KALEIDOSCOPE KINGDOM
Visiting Nazarene Worship in Unfamiliar Places
by Fletcher L. Tink

NAZARENE YOUTH GOES INTERNATIONAL
Adults and Youth Making a Difference Around the World
by Gary Sivewright

✽ ✽ ✽

NEW ADULT MISSION EDUCATION CURRICULUM
Living Mission

From the Ends of the Earth

The Growing Movement of Missionaries
from Non-Western Cultures

Ellen Decker

Nazarene Publishing House
Kansas City, Missouri

Copyright 2012
Nazarene Publishing House

ISBN 978-0-8341-2811-8

Printed in the
United States of America

Cover Design: Kevin Williamson
Interior Design: Sharon Page

Unless otherwise indicated, all Scripture quotations are taken from the *Holy Bible, New International Version*® (NIV®). Copyright © 1973, 1978, 1984 by Biblica, Inc.™ Used by permission of Zondervan. All rights reserved worldwide. www.zondervan.com.

Dedication

In 2000, the family and friends of Doris and Charles (Chuck) Gailey established a perpetual endowment in higher education for the training of cross-cultural missionaries from African countries. The Gailey Scholarship is in honor of their lifetime commitment to the worldwide proclamation of the gospel of Jesus Christ and their understanding that God calls missionaries from every nation—even "from the ends of the earth" (Psalms 61:2).

At Chuck's retirement from a twenty-one year career training missionaries at Nazarene Theological Seminary, Dr. Harold Raser said: "The importance of language acquisition, the importance of being able to distinguish between the gospel and cultural forms, concepts like 'indigenization' and 'contextualization'—thinking about the Church and mission in a more global way rather than 'us' and 'them'—these and many more vital developments in evangelical thinking about mission found their way into Nazarene practice through the influence of Dr. Chuck Gailey."

And so, to my extraordinary missionary parents, whose lives taught me to respect the dignity and worth of individuals from every culture, and who seemed to embody "globalization" long before the rest of the world was aware of it—this book is for you.

Contents

Acknowledgments	9
Author's Note	10
Prologue: The Beginning of the End	11
1. Until the End	15
2. Happy Endings	26
3. The Means to an End	35
4. At the End of the Day	42
5. Faithful to the End	52
6. Book Ends: Mission and Theology	60
7. The Mission Never Ends	67
8. No End in Sight	77
Epilogue: Endless	85
A Call to Action: The Ending is Up To You	89
Notes	91

Acknowledgments

With gratitude to all the missionaries in this book who allowed me to share their stories, and for their graciousness and patience with multiple languages and deadlines.

Special thanks to Isabela Thomazelli, a gifted young lady from Brazil. She translated three chapters and multiple e-mails into—and out of—Spanish and Portuguese. Her great efficiency and evident joy serving the Lord made working with her a real pleasure.

Thanks to missionary Paul Dayhoff for permission to use Salome's information from his book, *Living Stones in Africa*.

Thanks to Scott Brubaker for introducing me to Isabela; and to Elizabeth Musimbi and Wayne LaForce for e-mail assistance.

With appreciation to Jeannette Brubaker, for prayers and encouragement along the journey, and to Rev. Lynn Shaw, for perseverance and faith.

Siyabonga kakhulu to my amazing family—Hank, for thirty years of blessings—Kevin, Jay, Theresa, Ryan, Kendra, Alivia, and Ella—you are the very best. I am deeply thankful for you.

To my living Redeemer, Jesus Christ—in the end, I shall see you with my own eyes. (Job 19:25-27)

Author's Note

When I had the idea to write about cross-cultural missionaries from countries around the world, the focus of the book was how God calls people from the ends of the earth. Yet I was stunned to discover this wonderful fact: these eight families are themselves the fruit of Nazarene missions!

Both Carlos and Silvia Bauza received their missionary call through hearing missionaries speak. Gustavo Crocker was encouraged by a missionary to use his gifts for the Kingdom. The Obottes were inspired to ministry and also mentored by missionaries. Antonie Holleman's parents were introduced to the Nazarene Church through a missionary. Humberto Bullon's father and Luis Meza's father were saved by a missionary's evangelism. Jonas Mulate was saved while listening to a missionary. Last but not least, Samuel Yangmi is a third generation missionary.

These eight individuals and couples have planted more than five hundred churches, taught and mentored hundreds of pastors, and impacted thousands of people in dozens of countries. Be blessed as you see how God used the efforts of Nazarene world evangelism to impact these individuals—and how He is now multiplying their endeavors all around the world!

Prologue
The Beginning of the End

It is increasingly obvious that societies today are globally interconnected. Vast movements of people, instantaneous communication, and interdependence among the nations have all contributed to this global togetherness. Our denomination is also advancing as a worldwide entity. From the building of the Global Ministry Center and the weekly display of "Flags of the Nations" to the induction of the first non-North-American General Superintendent, we are truly becoming a church that is recognizing the reality that far more of our members now reside outside rather than inside North America.

Put into sheer numbers, the demographics look like this:
- In 1960 there were nearly six times as many members of the Church of the Nazarene in the US/Canada (318,597) as there were in world areas (54,055).
- By 2005, there were 649,170 members in US/Canada and 917,135 members in world areas.
- From 2006 to 2009, US/Canada members increased by 9,232 while world members increased by 261,856.

- If the same trends continue for the same length of time, by 2050 there will be 1.3 million members in USA/Canada but over 15.5 million members in other nations![1]

It should come as no surprise, then, that our Nazarene missionaries are coming from increasingly diverse world areas. The reality is that it is not just "us" sending to "them" anymore. As the body of Christ, we are not only called *to* all nations, we are called *from* all nations. As God said in Isaiah 41:9, "I took you from the ends of the earth; from its farthest corners I called you. I said, 'You are my servant'; I have chosen you and have not rejected you."

God is using spirit-filled Nazarenes to answer His call to go into the entire world as cross-cultural missionaries. There are tremendous advantages that can come from this growing movement of missionaries from non-Western cultures. After all, it is pretty difficult for Muslims to claim that Christianity is a Western religion if the person witnessing to them is from India or Ethiopia. As a result, we now have missionary training centers operating in several nations, including Argentina, Guatemala, Korea, Philippines, and Brazil, and our denominational missionaries come from thirty-nine countries.[2]

God's Word tells us that the gospel will be preached in the whole world as a testimony to all nations (Matt. 24:14). God loves the world, and He urgently wants to save the whole world! We are privileged to be alive at this time in human history. We are witnessing the beginning of the end as God calls obedient believers from all over the globe. This book is about a handful of them, their missionary callings, and how they are transforming communities and countries with the gospel. We need to hear the testimony of these Nazarene missionaries from the ends of the earth.

1
Until the End

The young girl in Argentina heard sad voices and thoughts in her mind. At the tender age of twelve she had already decided that life was not worth living. Wearily, she climbed to the roof of her home. The voices clamored, "Throw yourself off the roof, people are better off without you. *Jump!*" Then a sweet, small voice gently said, *Jesus loves you*. Suddenly, in that aching, lonely moment, she felt a palpable presence.

"I knew I wasn't alone anymore. I felt surrounded by Jesus' love. I felt overwhelmingly protected, as if angels covered me. I knew I needed Jesus as my Savior." Silvia climbed down off the roof that day, went to the Formosa Nazarene Church, and gave her life to the Lord. She's never looked back.

Carlos grew up in a Christian family—in fact it was his dad, Rev. Ramón Bauzá, who led Silvia to the Lord. As a young boy in Formosa, Argentina, Carlos was greatly impacted by missionaries who shared about the work in India and Madagascar. He was saved at six, baptized at ten, and sanctified at fourteen during a youth retreat. When he returned from that retreat, he and the teens from his dad's church planted a church in a neighboring town. Every week the youths rode their bikes nine miles round trip to share God's Word in that community. At nineteen, during one of the services at General Assembly in Indianapolis, Carlos received his call to be a missionary. He began ministering to the Toba Indians in South America.

Silvia was also greatly impacted by missionaries as she received her calling to be a missionary after Rev. Norman Howerton spoke at a youth camp. The first time she shared her testimony publicly, Pastor Felix Maldonado told Silvia, "Fan into flame the gift of God that is in you." That word confirmed her calling and gave her great encouragement. Her very first ministry was cross-cultural, also working with the Toba Indians. She and Carlos were asked to pastor that church of about seventy people and eventually fell in love and were married.

Less than a year after they were married they began to sense that God was preparing them for something. They decided to pray for a month. At the end of that month they happened to receive an invitation to pioneer Nazarene work in Paraguay. Carlos and Silvia looked at each other and said, "Yes!" Carlos, 22, and Silvia, 19, left everything: family, town, friends, church, home, and jobs to go on an adventure in a new culture. They didn't know what God was doing, but they knew they were traveling with Him, and that was enough.

The Bauzás served six years as volunteer missionaries in the northern part of Paraguay. The first three years were excruciatingly tough. They faced financial and health issues and were away from home for the first time. Their housing was very sparse and their well had dried up, leaving them without water for six months. Yet they persevered.

"During the next three years, the windows of heaven opened up. God blessed us in mighty ways. Two Work and Witness [W & W] teams came to build, and the two churches in Obrero and Don Bosco began to grow. Even though it is a very Catholic country, God gave us many opportunities to share the gospel, especially at funerals and weddings. We witnessed miracles and lives transformed by God's power. We had good jobs and enough to live on. It was going great!"

One day as Carlos was walking to church, he heard a voice within him, *Carlos, I brought you to Paraguay and I am taking you from Paraguay*. Once again the Bauzás began to pray. Soon after that, Silvia received a copy of *Trans African* magazine. On the front was the phrase, "Mozambique Miracle." Right away Carlos exclaimed, "We are going to Mozambique."

Carlos Bauzá in Mozambique

I thought he had gone nuts. We didn't have any connection to Mozambique at all, it was just impossible that we would ever go there. But we began to talk about Mozambique over the next few days. We read about it and soon discovered that Portuguese was the official language. We could hardly believe it—for the last several months we had been hosting some Brazilian pastors and we had been learning Portuguese! We began to pray earnestly for Mozambique. It was like a magnet that drew our attention and our hearts.

A few months later Carlos approached Dr. Bruno Radi and told him they had been praying for Mozambique and felt God wanted them to go. Dr. Radi began to cry. "Carlos, I have received five faxes from the Africa Regional Director, begging me to send two couples who know Portuguese to Mozambique right away."

Before they knew it, the Bauzás were at the airport headed for Mozambique.

> As I looked back at my family waving to us in the airport, it hit me that it would be years before I saw them. Jesus reminded me of His promise, "Everyone who has left houses or brothers or sisters or father or mother or children or fields for my sake will receive a hundred times as much and will inherit eternal life" (Matt. 19:29). Still, we cried a lot on the plane, as if our family umbilical cord had been cut. But when we arrived in Africa, there was the area director, Dr. Ken Walker, with a broad smile on his face and arms opened wide. They received us with much love and we soon realized: God gave us family in Africa too.

Adapting to a new culture is not always easy. Every place is different and missionaries have to respect the culture and the customs while at the same time learning the boundaries of behavior and language. Besides Spanish, English, and Portuguese, the Bauzás have tried to learn at least a few phrases in each of the eight major dialects spoken in their province. Coming from a modest background has helped them

Carlos Bauzá helping unload a wheelchair

adapt to the Mozambican culture, which is generally quite poverty-stricken.

Our kids have greatly helped to break down cultural barriers. Tamara was four when we moved here. When we went visiting, it would take her only about five minutes to find lots of friends to play with. They created inventive games from sticks, dust, leaves, coconut shells, plates, and make-believe food made from mud. When we visited the prison, the women inmates loved to see her and hold her since they missed their own children so much. After Sabrina and

Gabriela were born it became more challenging to travel with Carlos, but they have always been a key part of our ministry here in Mozambique. And even though we have brought part of our cultures with us—Argentinean tea and Paraguayan soup—we find that the Mozambican culture and foods have become integrated in our lives, especially in our children.

Fourteen years ago when the Bauzás arrived in northern Mozambique, their degrees in theology came in handy since the leadership fell squarely on their shoulders. It was a race every week to visit the churches and villages to show the *JESUS* Film, baptize, dedicate children, administer communion, and perform weddings—often all in the same service! Today each of the four districts has an ordained elder as district superintendent. There are area coordinators, *JESUS* Film teams, and ordained pastors teaching lay pastors through extension programs. The churches have grown from 86 to 254, and the Bauzás are encouraging orphan feeding and disaster relief compassionate ministries.

Many of the churches were made of mud and straw, making them susceptible to leaks and collapsing. Over the years, the Bauzás have strategically built eighteen churches from welded iron, donating the metal if the churches provide labor. Each church costs seven to twenty thousand dollars, depending on the size. Their goal is to build more churches if funds become available, as the spiritual growth is exploding.

Sometimes that growth has come through unusual circumstances. On a six hour trip to Derre, approximately 150 miles away, the truck was packed with *JESUS* Film equipment—generator, clothing, water, food, emergency lights, extra diesel, and four pastors. On the way they took refuge under a tree from the blazing sun. A truck broke down nearby and the driver begged them to take a baby's coffin and the parents to Derre. The coffin was placed over the *JESUS* Film equipment and the parents squished into a very tight space. When they arrived in Derre they discovered that the dead baby was one of the government authorities' grandsons. In appreciation for their efforts, the town gave the team permission to show the *JESUS* Film as well as land to build a Nazarene church. One dollar sealed the deal, and today there is a thriving church there!

The growth has also come with a price. The Bauzá family has suffered twenty-three malaria cases in their family. Gabriela almost died at five months old, saved by an emergency flight to Zimbabwe. At two years old, she was in a South African hospital, along with her father, fighting her fourth bout with malaria. Silvia watched as her baby struggled with pain and fever and then slipped into a coma.

Gabriela Bauzá with a friend in Mozambique

I was praying desperately by Gaby's bed when a lady came up to me and asked if she could pray for us. When she was done she looked me in the eye and quoted Isaiah 43:1-3: "But now, this is what the Lord says—he who created you, O Jacob, he who formed you, O Israel: 'Fear not, for I have redeemed you; I have summoned you by name, you are mine. When you pass through the waters, I will be with you; and when you pass through the rivers, they will not sweep over you. When you walk through the fire, you will not be burned; the flames will not set you ablaze. For I

Feeding children in Mozambique

am the LORD, your God, the Holy One of Israel, your Savior.'" A great peace flooded my soul, and I knew my family was going to be okay.

Even though the Bauzás still face many challenges, such as Tamara needing to return to Argentina for a good high school education, they realize there are many around them who have far greater needs.

Once when I was serving food in Tete, an elderly man struggled to come over. He was so thin and emaciated he could hardly walk. Yet when he reached me he thanked us for giving him food so he can return to work in the plantations.

Another great sadness is AIDS. A young family who recently graduated from seminary all died from AIDS within a year. We have had several pastors who have passed away from malaria, measles, AIDS, and tuberculosis. It is hard to not be able to help more. We so wish that we had the funds to create training centers for various professions so that pastors and church members can learn a trade to earn a living. The needs are so vast.

Yet far more than the physical needs, the greatest need is finding people who have a calling and a passion to reach the lost just as Jesus did. The mission field is enormous and the harvest is plentiful, but the laborers are few. We can assure you that in spite of the challenges, there is no better place than the center of God's will. Being a missionary is not just a job, it is a ministry until the end of our lives.

Message to the global Church: Thank you for the opportunity to serve and for the privilege of being a missionary. Thank you for trusting in us and helping us as we work to advance the ministry for His glory.

2
Happy Endings

Dr. David Livingstone was a Scottish missionary, doctor, and explorer who traveled across one-third of the African continent, opening the heart of Africa to missions. When he finally died of malaria at age sixty in Zambia, he was found kneeling by his bed where he had drawn his final breaths in prayer. His life motto had been, "Fear God and work hard."[3]

American Rev. Harmon Schmelzenbach pioneered the work for the Church of the Nazarene in Swaziland. In spite of multiple setbacks, including poor health and the death of four of his children, Harmon ministered for twenty-one years without a furlough. He died ministering in his beloved Swaziland.

Dr. Livingstone and Rev. Schmelzenbach's lives were our inspiration to become missionaries. Hellen and I could not get over the fact that these people, who were not Africans, came to seek lost Africans. Even though they knew they were so much more susceptible to malaria and other diseases here, they came and gave their lives. So when we looked around and saw fellow Africans dying in sin, we asked ourselves, "How can we do any less?" White missionaries from across the oceans did their part to take the holiness message to the lost and dying. Now it is our turn.

While these were the men whose life-stories inspired Rev. Wellington and Hellen Obotte to say yes to God's calling on their lives, they were also influenced by many modern-day missionaries in Africa. Individuals like Rev. Harmon Schmelzenbach III, Dr. Ken Walker, Dr. Charles Gailey, Dr. Geneva Silvernail, and Dr. Richard Zanner were all instrumental in the Obotte's missionary calling.

It was while studying at Nazarene Theological College in Siteki, Swaziland, that God spoke specifically to the Obottes through Isaiah 6:8, "Then I heard the voice of the Lord saying, 'Whom shall I send? And who will go for us?' and I said, 'Here am I. Send me!'" After completing his Bachelor's in theology, Wellington went on to receive a Master's in Religion from Africa Nazarene University in Kenya.

The Obottes were the first African missionaries to be officially commissioned as global missionaries by the Church. In some ways it has been a benefit for the Obottes, allowing them to go into places where white missionaries cannot easily go, such as the predominantly Muslim island of Zanzibar. In other ways,

Wellington, Hellen, Juliet, Jerald Obotte

the challenges they faced were huge, especially when it came to people's expectations.

We are black global missionaries. Not what one expects in the Nazarene Church, even in Africa. The very first time we went to a zone meeting as missionaries in Tanzania, they knew that a missionary was going to speak to the crowd of 150 there. The service kept continuing on and on, and finally the worship leader said, "Let's stop and pray for our missionaries, perhaps they have had traveling difficulties." I sent a message up to the worship leader, telling him the missionary was already here in the congregation. He looked out over us, but not seeing a white person in the crowd, interpreted the note to mean that the missionary was still coming. So they had us sing some more songs until finally the worship leader said, "If there is a missionary representative among us, would you please come to the platform?" I stood and went to the front. After greeting them, I took the opportunity to explain what a missionary is and how God can call anyone in the world to be a missionary. The sad thing is that after this conference, the church lost thirty out of the forty pastors that attended. They were so used to having white missionaries that they thought the Nazarene Church was abandoning them.

Since African missionaries are a relatively new idea in the Nazarene Church, the Obottes have spent much of the last fifteen years teaching the congregations to support mission work. They have repeatedly encouraged the churches to recognize that winning souls does not depend on money. Yes, money is needed, but it is not the solution.

In spite of these challenges, God brought about many happy endings during their eleven years in Tanzania. Many of those thirty pastors returned to the Nazarene Church. Wellington mentored and groomed ten pastors to encourage the leadership of national District Superintendents. Wellington also founded and managed a Nazarene high school that began with fifty students and is now teaching five hundred students. Both of the Obottes were heavily involved in evangelism and the work multiplied from one district to three. More than 250 viable church plants were started, 180 of them through nine teams of the *JESUS* Film ministry, which Hellen coordinated.

"When we visited one village to show the *JESUS* Film, two ladies got particularly excited. They went around telling people, 'Come and see Jesus, he is speaking our language of Kiswahili!' They would shout out to everyone, 'We can hear Him clearly, He is speaking to us, we must follow Him!' That night over three hundred people knelt down and cried when they saw that they killed a good man who was a healer. One hundred and fifty received Jesus as Lord. A church was started here with 110 in attendance. It grew to 260 members within a year."

The Lord just kept blessing His work across Tanzania, despite obstacles. Once, Wellington went with a colleague to show the *JESUS* Film in a remote village. Over fifty people were saved, but after the showing it began raining. Thinking it would soon end, Wellington and Tim started back home in their small car. The now-torrential rain continued until the car got stuck in the mud and would not move. Tim and Wellington spent the night in the cramped vehicle and had to hire a coffee farmer's tractor to pull them out.

Besides evangelism, Hellen Obotte has a heart for helping pastors' wives learn to read, write, and handle basic math and sewing. "Rosa [this name and others from similar stories have been changed] had never had any formal education when she began coming to our ladies meetings. I began teaching her the alphabet. After just three months, Rosa had begun reading and was writing her name. As she continued to come, she began writing more extensively. Then she began attending the pastors' extension classes and assisting her husband in teaching Sunday School at their church. Today Rosa is teaching other ladies to read and write."

Hellen also brought in stones and began teaching the ladies to count. From there she worked up to basic math concepts and business principles of handling money. Some of the ladies pooled their money to purchase a sewing machine, which saves them significant money on clothing. The biggest challenges for women's ministry are the lack of transportation, funds to begin small business start-ups, and the general task of raising children.

Hellen can empathize with the women on the challenge of raising children. In Tanzania education is done in the primary language of Swahili. Because the Obottes wanted their children to learn English, they sent their children to boarding schools in Kenya. The separation was hard on all the family, but the

Obottes learned to trust God on a new level and to rediscover His faithfulness to them.

The Obottes always carry with them the Kenyan "Harambee spirit," which means that everyone must pull together, work together, and help out. When they see the transformed lives, they know it has been worth it all.

> I once went to preach at a homestead that hosted a witchdoctor. After preaching, the wife of the village headman got saved; a few months later, her husband was saved. About a year later, the witchdoctor came to the Lord. The witchdoctor eventually became the pastor of the church that was started in that village. He became influential and was instrumental in planting churches in the Mugonzi area of Tanzania. After he planted fifteen churches, he became the zone leader of that area. It's just amazing to watch God at work.

Wellington, who speaks English, Kiswahili, SiSwati, Luo, Luhya, and Luganda, realized he would have to learn another language, Chichewa, when they were assigned to The Republic of Malawi in 2007. But, he consoled himself with the thought that the church had been there since 1957. *How difficult can it be?* he wondered. *We will just go and give a little guidance and help with some strategies to get them to the next level.*

Much to their surprise, they discovered that not only would they would have to get back to the basics, their duties as missionaries in Malawi would be quite varied. Hellen coordinates the Child Sponsorship Program and also continues her work with pastors' wives and women's ministries. Wellington works with the five districts in evangelism and leadership strategies, oversees Nazarene Compassionate Ministries (NCM) and W & W ministries, teaches part time at Nazarene Theological College, and holds annual holiness seminars and other meetings throughout the year.

> A significant victory we had recently was in one of our districts that has not yet achieved regular status. For a long time it seemed hard to get the understanding across that we must be creative in organizing events and raising our own funding. This is an enormous challenge in Malawi, which is one of the world's ten poorest countries with an average annual income of just $160 USD. It was a tremendous feeling of satisfaction for the district to host its own Pastors and Spouses Retreat. Everyone stayed in a modest guest house, but they did it!"

As they look to the future, the Obottes have big dreams for Malawi. They want to intensify evangelism across the country and to disciple leaders who will carry the torch for the next generation. There is still a huge need for theological training, since there are many churches that lack trained pastors. Equally pressing is teaching local churches to take care of their pastors by helping them to raise crops, among other things.

The biggest need is empowerment. We need to teach our missionaries and pastors, especially those who are ministering in poorer countries, skills that can be beneficial to the people they are ministering to. There also needs to be a deliberate plan and strategy about ownership. One good thing about being black African missionaries to other Africans is that there is a greater possibility that they will take ownership, rather than look to a white missionary to do it for them. We are inspired when we see people accepting Christ, being called to ministry, and being trained to take over church responsibilities. But we really light up when we see that some pastors and church members have truly started to realize that they are Church of the Nazarene, too.

Message to the global Church: It is our prayer that the Nazarene Church will encourage the training of non-American missionaries in missions. We are thankful for the opportunity to serve as your global missionaries.

3
The Means to an End

He was raised in the home of the first Nazarene pastor—and later the first Nazarene District Superintendent—of the Dutch district. As a young lad of seven he accepted the call of Jesus. Ever since then, Antonie had a burning passion to be a pastor. He prayed earnestly for God to not only bless that calling, but also to multiply his ministry many times over.

Wilma was raised in a Dutch Reformed family. At nineteen she experienced a conversion to a deeper faith and found a new home in the Church of the Nazarene. It was during a Nazarene summer camp that she met Antonie and they discovered a mutual love and call to ministry. They married in 1984. Wilma earned a degree in nursing while Antonie graduated in theology from the University of Leiden and was later ordained in 1992. Rev. Holleman pastored the Rotterdam Nazarene Church for seven years while Wilma worked with the youth. She later joined the faculty at European Nazarene College (EuNC) where Antonie now serves as the academic dean.

Antonie and Wilma Holleman

Pastoring the Rotterdam Church was a wonderful experience and can definitely be seen as preparation for our missionary work. When we were invited to EuNC in Switzerland, we made the decision almost immediately in response to God's clear calling, and sensed a great peace. Many Dutch people—like us—tend to be entrepreneurs, open to new things, and lovers of freedom and change. At the same time, we knew where we were going to, we had visited the school many times, and we already knew German. In many ways we did not feel like we were missionaries; we were simply being obedient to God's call; just instead of serving a congregation, we were serving a college.

However, it wasn't long for reality to set in. Though not geographically distant compared to many missionary assignments, it is in many ways a different world. The Hollemans are only able to return to the Netherlands a couple of times a year, and that is usually for church-related responsibilities. All of their extended family lives in the Netherlands and they miss most of the family gatherings. Yet, after fifteen years as missionaries, they also recognize there is a growing disconnect with their Dutch heritage.

> We live on the border between Germany and Switzerland. We do not feel Swiss or German deep in our hearts, yet when we are back in the Netherlands we do not feel we belong there either, even though there is still a lot that is familiar. Many of the missionaries we work with are American, yet comparatively we are very European. After all these years we realize we will never fully become like the Germans or the Swiss, yet we will probably never again feel completely at home in our own country. We wonder about the future as well: where will our children live or study? Germany? Switzerland? The Netherlands? Or perhaps even another country? These uncertainties are the consequences of our decision to

leave our country and serve at the college. Yet we feel at home at the college, which is also a mix of different cultures. It has become our God-given family and the group we belong to. This Christian community creates our identity beyond family ties, nationality, and culture. What a blessing from God, our provider!

Because of their unique location on a border, the Holleman family lives cross-culturally every day. They know Dutch, German, and English. Their two children, Frank and Corianne, also speak Swiss German. They all switch easily from one language to another and have actually created their own language in the home, a mixture of Dutch, German, and English.

Antonie acknowledges the tremendous opening that God has provided through the multinational work of the Church of the Nazarene. With this global network of the Church, Antonie has the opportunity to serve churches in all of Europe and is not limited to one congregation in the Netherlands. EuNC has provided Wilma the opportunity to teach New Testament Greek and coordinate the internship program. She has also enrolled in the Master's of Divinity online program from Northwest Nazarene University. Antonie and Wilma are truly partners in ministry.

As a pastor preparing future pastors at EuNC, Antonie received his multiplying ministry. EuNC is a professional school of ministry specifically designed to educate people for Christian service and to lay a solid foundation in them for ministry. Through transformational education that reflects our Wesleyan theological heritage, EuNC enables students to participate in the mission of God as they serve local communities of faith. The international faith community of EuNC is not only committed to authenticity and integrity, it is committed to allowing its core curriculum to adapt to the cultural context and specific ministry needs of each of the seventeen countries across Europe and the former Soviet Union where the college has learning centers.

In 2004, EuNC began a seven-year project called "Moving Forward." Antonie says this is a strategy that outlines the priority of the future as being "one multicultural and multinational school with one campus and many teaching locations in various European countries, with the goal of exposing the students to the best of residential and extension education."

> This has been a dream in the making, an opportunity to build a school that is relevant to the twenty-first century. It is our hope that we will contribute to a rejuvenation of Christianity through education. You see, for many people education is simply the accumulation of knowledge. At EuNC, we respectfully disagree. We do not believe that knowledge is neutral in-

formation. Knowledge does something to the learner—it influences our perspectives, values, and even our actions. As Paul indicates in Romans 12:2, theological knowledge renews the mind and transforms people. As such, EuNC is convinced that the education we provide needs to contribute to a revival of genuine Christianity in order to restore the role of the Church as a transformational agency in society. Then, as the rejuvenated Church, we can fully participate in God's mission in the world.

One of the concerns with modern day missions is that it can become too much about numbers, organization, and structure. While some of this is perhaps unavoidable, one way that the Hollemans bring mission to a local level is through one-on-one mentoring with their students, the future leaders of the Nazarene Church in Europe. "Being transparent and developing deep and meaningful relationships is highly valued in Dutch culture and is one of the Dutch characteristics we can contribute to the lives of our students. Some of them who come to EuNC have not been encouraged by their families to pursue their calling. Being a friend and coach to them is one of the most fulfilling aspects of our ministry. Every time we see a former student ordained and serving a church as a pastor, we are proud of them and thankful for what God has done in their lives."

Because of his position, Antonie travels throughout Europe. He was in Albania when he spoke with me and answered my questions. He remarked that the greatest blessing of his travels is the friendliness of the people in Nazarene churches and the sense of their love and passion for God. "We are constantly being inspired to find ways to restore the church of Christ in authentic ministry. Perhaps the best way each of us can do that is to be more receptive to what God wants to do in and through us."

Message to the global church: Let us be more sincere and less self-congratulatory. Let us seek God more.

4
At the End of the Day

In 1984 I was returning home from church at night when I saw a strange man. He had drunk too much and had been robbed, even of his clothes. Many parts of his body were wounded and bleeding. When he asked for my help, I was scared. I took him to a policeman and asked him to take the man to the hospital. When I got home, I couldn't sleep. When I closed my eyes I kept seeing that man's face, pleading for help. I prayed and went back to the place where the policeman was. I couldn't find him. Right there on the street I began weeping and asking God to forgive me. I told him that if He ever gave me another opportunity to help someone, I would do everything in my power to help.

Since that dark night of crisis, God has used Dr. Luis Meza and his wife, Clarita, to touch the lives of countless hurting and suffering people through a variety of ministries. Luis, who holds degrees in accounting, theology, education, missiology, and ministry, has held down multiple positions at a time. He served as a bi-vocational pastor, Compassion International's coordinator in Peru, South American (SAM) Regional NCM Coordinator, president of the South America Nazarene Theological Seminary, and coordinator of the Nazarene work in Colombia.

I am so blessed to have been born into a Christian family. My father accepted Jesus through the ministry of missionary Rev. Clyde Golliher. From a young age I attended the Church of the Nazarene in Talara, Peru. The lives of the missionaries were inspiring and challenging to me. When I think of the Golliher, Gray, Douglas, Garman, John, and Brunson families, I thank God for their impact on my life and that of so many others in Peru. I love the Nazarene Church! It has given me the gospel through the sending of missionaries. It has encouraged me through theory and practice. In theory, for it taught me through Nazarene Theological Seminary. In practice, for it has given me a place to serve God—first in [Nazarene Youth International] (NYI) in my local church, then at the district, national, regional, and global levels. David Livingstone once expressed how I feel at the end of each day: "Anything that I do for the Lord—even if I offered my own life as a sacrifice—wouldn't be enough to pay for what He has done for me." Being God's servant as a missionary is an undeserved privilege. I thank God for His great love and mercy towards me, and for the support and understanding of my wonderful family.

For the last twenty years, the Mezas have served sacrificially as missionaries. Their children were born in different countries—Denisse in Peru, Luis Jr. in Ecuador, and Daniel in Costa Rica. Like most missionary kids, they were raised with limited contact with their extended family. Perhaps the biggest challenge, however, was confronting the perceptions about compassionate ministries when Luis first began as the SAM NCM Coordinator. Since it was a new ministry in the Church's infrastructure, some colleagues thought it was an unnecessary addition. Some viewed it as a "second-class" ministry or a way to "hook" people into the Church. Others viewed compassionate ministries as all about money.

God really helped us to have wisdom to know how to share the meaning of Christian compassion from a biblical standpoint. The Bible itself shows us a compassionate God who asks His people to be compassionate. Jesus is our example in Matthew 9:35, "Jesus went through all the towns and villages, teaching in their synagogues, preaching the good news of the kingdom and healing every disease and sickness." Com-

Luis Meza (r.), counseling in Brazil

passion is not all about what we do. At the end of the day, it is about who we are. It is about compassion as a lifestyle.

Luis is a strong believer that it's not all about programs.

> I once read that if you teach a church to create a program, they will create a program. But if you share a vision with them, there is no limit to what they can do with God's help! As I put this into practice over the last twenty years, I have seen ordinary people grasp God's vision and create great projects that benefited many. There are children's feeding programs in Peru, a medical clinic in Brazil, an irrigation system in

Ecuador, children's projects in Colombia, food programs for street people in Chile, and many, many other projects across South America because people caught the vision of living as God's compassionate people. The best projects don't depend on money. They depend on the vision that God gives, and the money follows from obedient hearts. We have a big Commission. We also have a big Commandment to love others, illustrated so beautifully through the Good Samaritan parable when Jesus commanded us to "go and do the same."

The Nazarene seminary in Ecuador has been training leaders to "go and do the same" for twenty-two years. At a compassionate ministry seminar Luis led in 1996, he remembers a pastor who brought a youth named Rodrigo. Rodrigo was extremely thin and there was evidence he had suffered a lot in his young life. Rodrigo shared a short testimony of how the pastor had found him living under a bridge. He got saved and the pastor was helping him quit drugs through a recovery program run by the church. A few years later, Rodrigo was called into ministry and attended the seminary where Luis was president.

> Seeing Rodrigo's change was a great delight. His face reflected peace and joy. He was literally transformed. He faithfully attended church with his wife Gladys and their two children, longing

to serve the Lord. Even though Rodrigo had not been able to finish high school, both he and Gladys worked hard, achieved good grades, and graduated from seminary. Rodrigo and Gladys returned to Colombia and planted a church. Many people in their neighborhood have come to know Christ as their personal Savior. Miracles have happened and they have had a tremendous impact on the community, like when a homosexual named Ivan became a Christian. He is now married and has a young son. Rodrigo's vision is a piece of land where we could build a recovery center for drug addicts.

Though God was doing great things at the seminary, Luis knew when he was asked to lead the Church's work in Colombia that it was the right step, even though there was clear and present danger. Colombia was almost synonymous with cocaine, heroin, guerilla warfare, and terrorism. Ten years ago there were more than three thousand kidnappings a year and more people killed than in the Middle East.

One thing we have definitely learned as global missionaries is that we don't need to fulfill the call on our own. It is something God will do through us. It's interesting that when God called Abraham, He didn't call him to do something. He called him to dwell in His presence. That doesn't mean we don't do anything, but it does mean we need to be very sensitive to God's voice and to dwell in His presence enough to know what He wants. Even in very challenging times we have peace in our hearts as we experience His presence. On a very practical level, it has been an advantage to be Latin missionaries so we are not readily a target for kidnapping.

Even so, one pastor and two NYI presidents have been killed. Another pastor was kidnapped two times by terrorist groups, and several churches have suffered attacks. Perhaps it should come as no surprise that Luis turned to the Book of Job for God's promise for Colombia, "But if you will look to God and plead with the Almighty, if you are pure and upright, even now he will rouse himself on your behalf and restore you to your rightful place" (Job 8:5-6). They have begun a national prayer and fasting movement across the country, and almost all of the Nazarene churches have prayer meetings at 5 o'clock every morning.

Colombia needs to be transformed and healed. We want the church to be salt and light. We want to see evangelism become a lifestyle among Colombian Nazarenes. We long for revival, not just in the neighborhoods, but in entire cities. We yearn to see a church eager to be in God's presence and compassionate toward hurting people. Historically, the Nazarene Church was founded by compassionate leaders to reach the lost and the suffering. We are returning to our roots and the basic Christian principles of prayer, fasting, and the revelation of God's Word. And as the Church remembers the secret of prayer in relationship with God, He is responding and doing wonderful things among us!

Indeed He is. From 2002 to 2009, membership exploded from just over 5,000 to 14,500. More than 20,000 are in attendance every Sunday in the 74 Nazarene churches across Colombia. In the beginning, the challenge was a lack of growth. Now the challenge is to find enough space, with many churches going to two or three services every Sunday (Cali, Colombia, has five Sunday morning worship services with approximately 2,000 people at each one). The Holy Spirit is changing lives and drawing people to Him!

Francisco is one of those people. He was part of a drug cartel, working as a bodyguard for a drug lord. He was tasked with murdering so many people he can't remember how many he's killed. One of his bosses lived near a Nazarene church and Francisco frequently noticed the sign. His wife started attending church and became saved. Shortly after that, Francisco decided to go to church. From the moment he stepped into that Nazarene church, his life was changed. He became a Christian that day and left his old life behind. Shortly afterwards, the drug cartel's leader was arrested and many of his cartel were murdered. Today Francisco tells his powerful testimony and has led many of his neighbors and friends to the Lord. He leads several Bible studies and his joy is contagious.

Omar is another whose life was changed. He is a national radio show director in Colombia. He didn't believe in God, mistreated his employees, wasted his income on parties and women, and had a marriage in shambles. One day he was asked to interview Charly Cardona, a famous musician. Omar did not know Charly was a Christian and the interview was to be held in a Nazarene church. At the church, Omar was invited to a church retreat. He doesn't know why he accepted, since he thought pastors were just crooks after people's money. During the last session of the retreat, God spoke to Omar in a powerful way. He wept for a full hour as he accepted God's forgiveness and grace. Today Omar is back with his wife Adriana. He is an exemplary husband and father and they all faithfully attend church.

There are still many rivers to be crossed, walls to be pulled down, and barriers to overcome in Colombia. Yet there is a promised land to be conquered, and Luis senses a new promise from the Lord: "Ask of Me, and I will make the nations your inheritance, the ends of the earth your possession" (Psalm 2:8). This is already happening! Where Satan once had a

Luis Meza (r.) helping a little boy through compassionate ministries in Brazil

grip, God is manifesting His Spirit—in the ends of the earth.

Message to the global Church: Joshua's call happened over two thousand years ago, yet this is still the call for the Nazarene Church in the twenty-first century: "Consecrate yourselves, for tomorrow the LORD will do amazing things among you" (Josh. 3:5). As a one-hundred-year-old-plus denomination, it is a great time to consecrate ourselves and seek God's presence, so that every Church of the Nazarene will become what one of our founders, Phineas Bresee, referred to as "a holy fire place."

5
Faithful to the End

Rev. Samuel Yangmi is a Christian today because of missions and sacrificial living. His birth mother was a Lisu refugee in Burma who fled China during the Mao Revolution. When she discovered they would be forced to return to communist China, she gave up five-month-old Samuel for adoption by missionary Drema Esther Morse Yangmi. Drema Esther, herself a Tibetan, had been adopted by missionaries Russell and Gertrude Morse during their forty-five years in the mountainous area of Tibet. A decade after Samuel's adoption, the Morse family was forced to flee over rugged terrain, including Drema Esther, who was eight months pregnant at the time. For the next six years the family hid and ministered in Hidden Valley, where several creative access countries meet.[5]

Eventually, to escape persecution, the family immigrated to the United States through India. At the age of sixteen, Samuel arrived in Missouri and began sixth grade. He quickly caught on and entered Ozark Christian College just three years later. While

Samuel Yangmi with his mother, Drema Esther

attending college he served as a youth pastor for three years. While it was tempting to remain in the West, Samuel had heard the story of his adoption and had a longing to reach his people in Asia with the gospel. Samuel then returned and climbed mountains, evangelizing from village to village in the unreached areas of northern Thailand for the next four years. There he met and married a beautiful young Lahu Christian lady, Lumae, in 1978. Their marriage was pre-arranged according to Asian customs. Two years later they returned to the United States for Samuel to earn a degree in international agri-business from MidAmerica Nazarene University.

Upon graduation, Samuel and Lumae returned to Thailand. Samuel began using his agricultural knowledge to assist opium growers in switching to coffee, tea, and other crops. "We had ten villages switch to other crops. One village began growing garlic, but they needed assistance. We were able to help them through a microfinance project. The crop took off, and the average income for the people went from about $400 annually to $1,000 or more annually. Best of all, the people were faithful in tithing. The result is that their church is now supporting its pastor and standing on its own two feet. Many of the other churches in northern Thailand are trying to follow their example."

Samuel's breakthrough with the Red Lahu tribe in Thailand began with Ca Suh, a witchdoctor. Ca Suh had a vision of two men walking near his home. They told him the true God was going to visit him. Shortly after, he was shown the biblical story through a View-Master set. The first photo he saw was of Aaron and Moses, the same two men he had seen in his vision. Ca Suh immediately made the connection with his vision and converted to Christianity. Today Ca Suh is one of eleven ordained pastors on the Northern Thailand District. This was followed by the conversion of an entire village called Ban Mai Pattana in northern Thailand. The village decided to give up worshipping evil spirits and converted to Christianity. To have the whole village, including the headman, decide that it was time to change their religion was an historic event among the Red Lahu people.

Samuel, who speaks Thai, English, Lisu, Lahu, Burmese, Kachin, and some Chinese, sometimes finds himself in challenging language situations.

> I was returning from English services in the States to a convention in Thailand. Fortunately, my wife was in the congregation and called out to me that I needed to speak in the correct language. It was only then that I realized I was speaking Lisu to a Lahu audience! Also, since our marriage was largely prearranged in the Asian custom, when we got married we did not have a mutual language to communicate to each other. Our communication skills were about fifteen percent. You'll be happy to know that after more than thirty-two years of marriage, we are now up to about sixty percent!

Not only does he have to juggle many languages, Samuel also wears many hats. Although he turned over the Northern Thailand District and its first one thousand members to its first national district superintendent, Samuel is now the district superintendent of a new pioneer district called Northern Mekong.

Sam and Lumae Yangmi

The district covers work in four creative access countries and overlaps in training with Vietnam. Samuel also coordinates NCM work in creative access nations in the area, functions as a W & W host, serves on the board of Nazarene Education for Southeast Asia, and is serving in an advisory role to Northern Thailand in its pursuit of reaching regular district status.

Samuel concentrates his efforts on planting churches, organizing districts through mentoring the leadership, and translating the Nazarene Manual into the Lisu and Lahu languages. He is also working toward establishing more Bible colleges for spiritual leaders in that part of the world. Because he remembers his own childhood of hardship and poverty, one of Samuel's passions is for the children of the three orphanages he and Lumae have begun through NCM. The Mae Tang Tribal Home in Thailand, Heavenly Grace in Burma, and an orphanage for Lisu children in China are producing our future leaders in those areas.

I was once caught by the secret service in China. But when they realized that I was with the church that began the orphanage established with the permission of the Lisu King, the boss of the secret service just asked me to come to his area and start another orphanage! Even in these moments of risk, the most that I can do is the least I can do—in comparison of what Christ did for me on that cross. This ministry is not all about us, it's all about Him. It also helps to be Asian in areas where standing out like a Caucasian missionary would not be a good idea.

One challenging aspect of ministry for the Yangmis is that they serve in an area where ministries and opportunities to reach unchurched people groups are expanding, but at a time when budget cuts are frequent. "We are under tremendous constraints today like I have never seen before. At the same time, doors are opening to new areas and people groups. The local churches here are doing what they can to help our districts be able to plant new churches—an incredible eighty percent of the members of Nazarene churches in northern Thailand are tithing—yet international financial cutbacks make it difficult to take the gospel through those open doors."

In spite of the constraints, Samuel has seen God doing incredible things in the country of his birth.

> There are thousands of Lisu people excited about the Church of the Nazarene that emphasizes the doctrine of holiness. It seems like a spark of fire has begun lighting up the mountains of these creative access nations. We have more than three thousand members; we are beginning to teach the course of study to pastors, and the district structure is beginning to take shape. Pray for us as we work in these gospel-resistant areas, as we make disciples who can make disciples. Pray for us to be faithful to the end.

One personally thrilling moment for Samuel was when he went to Burma to take in ninety-two members for the Church of the Nazarene, only to discover his birth mother was one of them! Although his birth father had passed away, at age thirty-eight Samuel was blessed to meet his birth mother—and welcome her into the Nazarene family. Sadly, although his birth parents had gone on to have six more sons, five of them had died, mostly from malaria. Living in a country where hardship is a way of life and she struggles to purchase a pair of oxen for plowing their rice field, Sam's birth mother has nevertheless taken in her five sons' orphans and is raising them for the Lord.

"I am truly blessed to know that my birth mother and my own children are in the Church. None of them are outside of Christ! This is such a joy for Lumae and me. Since all our children and grandchildren are now in the United States, our hearts are tugged a bit more each time we go back to Thailand. We often have to remind ourselves that we are really just passing through, and our citizenship and permanent home together is in heaven!"

Samuel Yangmi knows God is watching over him. God spared Samuel from growing up in a communist regime by forcing him out of his country as a child. He helped Samuel survive for six years on the run in Hidden Valley, where he was forced to eat monkeys from a leech-infested jungle, where a friend was killed by a tiger. God has spared him over and over as he traveled in dangerous areas of the world.

So why stay in the U.S. in a cushy job when he can return to the very nations that tried to eliminate him—and tell them about Jesus? After all, that is simply being faithful to the end.

Message to the global Church: Brace for change. Impact your world for Christ by getting involved with all your heart and mind in Kingdom-building work. Look steadfast on the face of Jesus.

6
Book Ends: Mission and Theology

Dorothy, the child of a Scottish mother and British father, was born as a missionary kid in Huancayo, Peru. Though she went to boarding school in Wales and still follows the Manchester United Football team in England, Peru holds a special place in her heart. It was there that she met and married the love of her life, Humberto, a young man who grew up in a Nazarene home. Together they were inspired by Rev. John Mackay, a Scottish missionary to Peru. Rev. Mackay believes that missionaries should become a member of the community they are ministering to, earning them the right to be heard through specific services that meet distinct needs within the receiving culture. These might include the demonstration of authentic Christianity in action through medical, educational, or agricultural service. This gift of service then offers a platform through which the missionary can effectively proclaim his faith.

Humberto and Dorothy Bullon

Like Mackay, Humberto and Dorothy feel strongly that mission needs to be holistic in its approach. "It is evangelism, consistent discipleship, and sacrificial and informed service in the face of huge social problems that will help the Church grow in such a way that it changes the societies of our nations. This growth needs to be qualitative and authentic in nature. One way to do this is to have more coordination and cooperation between different Christian groups in order to work together for the advancement of the Kingdom of God as a united force."

From the very beginning of their ministry, Humberto and Dorothy have been involved in this cooperative effort. Dorothy, who became a registered nurse and certified midwife in London, began her ministry in a hospital near Cuzco, Peru. Later she felt called to reach university students and joined with InterVarsity Christian Fellowship (IVF), which is how she met Humberto. As an industrial engineer, Humberto was working for IVF as a project leader, training students and professionals to use their vocations for the needy in Peru.

Soon after getting married, Humberto and Dorothy became pastors of the Pueblo Libre Church of the Nazarene in Lima, Peru. After three years of pastoring and teaching at the University of Lima, Humberto began his PhD in Development Studies in Manchester, England. Upon his graduation in 1990, the Bullons applied to World Mission as missionaries. Because of their six combined postgraduate degrees and varied backgrounds, they were sent as missionaries to teach at the Seminario Nazareno de las Americas, which is our flagship accredited postgraduate seminary for Latin America.

One of the things that really thrills us is when we see our students enthusiastically serving as pastors or Christian leaders. Two of our best students have gone on to serve as presidents of Seminario Teologico Nazareno Sudamericano in Ecuador and of Seminario Teologico Nazareno Del Cono Sur in Argentina. We know that each course we teach is like a brick being built into their formation, and that our faculty, as a team, is putting these bricks into place. It is exciting to be a part of an institution whose goal is to comprehensively train servant leaders for the Nazarene Church of tomorrow. What a joy to see students doing really well and serving God with all their hearts!

Humberto and Dorothy not only teach at the seminary in Costa Rica, they have also taught in the Master's Degree extension program in all of the twelve centers and ten countries across Latin America. They have both served with NCM—Humberto as the Panama, Costa Rica, and Nicaragua coordinator for two years, and Dorothy as Child Sponsorship coordinator for the same countries for six years.

Besides their excellence in teaching, Humberto and Dorothy have continued their cooperative effort to build God's Kingdom. Dorothy launched an evangelical student group at the Catholic University in Lima, Peru, that is still continuing after more than twenty-five years. In Costa Rica she has served on the steering committee to develop the evangelical Alpha Course, which "teaches only the basic, biblical teachings that all Christians agree on,"[6] among the Catholic parishes. Humberto has served in the Latin American Theological Fellowship as the coordinator for Costa Rica and participated in the International Congress on World Evangelism in Switzerland. Both have published several books. One of Dorothy's, *Towards the Theology of Revival*, was published by CLIE, the largest publishing house for Christian books in Spanish. Humberto's three-volume set, *Christian Mission and Social Responsibility*, was published by Kairós.

For relaxation, the Bullons enjoy cooking. One of their favorite dishes is the Costa Rican Gallo Pinto, a breakfast dish of rice, black beans, red peppers, cilantro, scrambled eggs and cream cheese. Another favorite is from Peru, Papa a la Huancaina, which is an appetizer consisting of cold cooked potatoes, lettuce, corn on the cob, hardboiled eggs, aji (Peruvian chili pepper), special sauce, and cream crackers, all garnished with black olives. A dish they enjoy that is found in both cultures is ceviche, a raw fish marinated in lemon juice and served with raw onions, corn, cilantro, red peppers, chilies, and lettuce. While living in Costa Rica they have missed the Peruvian delicacies of roast guinea pig and alpaca steaks, but every Christmas Dorothy's British heritage is reveled with the serving of traditional Christmas pudding!

Though their lives have centered on academia, the Bullons have had their share of excitement. When Humberto was hosting a group of leaders from around the world for a project in Peru, a South Korean pastor, not used to the hairpin bends and bumpy roads, accidentally drove the car over the edge of a cliff. It flipped three times in the air before landing in a tree, but fortunately no one was seriously hurt. A farmer came along and said that the day before he had nearly cut down the tree, but for some reason had decided not to.

Another time, Humberto parked his car by a government building. Five minutes later a bomb placed by the Peruvian Tupac Amaru Guerilla movement went off. Humberto was fine, but the car was badly damaged. God's providence spared them once again when someone attempted to kidnap their two-year-old son, Daniel, in an Andean village marketplace. Daniel's four-year-old brother, David, immediately ran after the person and grabbed his brother back, causing the perpetrator to flee.

The Bullons are keenly aware of—and very thankful for—prayer support from around the world: from Loving, Interested Nazarenes Knowing and Sharing (LINKS) churches in the U.S., to churches across the United Kingdom and Peru, to the Tibás Nazarene Church in Costa Rica where they are currently members. While they love to return to Peru and England and have precious family and friends there, they have been joyfully surprised that they could give their hearts so fully to Costa Rica.

In retirement they plan to stay in Costa Rica for a few years, eventually moving to Peru. Their son David works in Peru with Innovation for Poverty Action. Daniel, an anthropologist, is working as a translator in Costa Rica. When asked what has inspired their missionary career, Dorothy replied thoughtfully, "A historical sense of participating in Christ's revolutionary process of the Kingdom of God, knowing that we are contributing to train the present and future generation of servants for the twenty-first century—not only through the teaching of classes, but also through the printed word—in the power of the Holy Spirit."

Message to the global Church: Get involved; give yourselves to God and His service. Go on mission trips to other countries to see where you might fit in. You will be spiritually stretched and discover gifts you never knew you had to serve the Kingdom of God and His justice.

7

The Mission Never Ends

Gustavo is the youngest of eight children. In the midst of an intense civil war in the 1970s in Guatemala, his oldest brother joined the revolutionary movement. When the death squads called for the eldest's assassination on his first wedding anniversary, he fled the country. In retaliation, on his second wedding anniversary, the repressive death troops killed one of Gustavo's other brothers "so the family would never forget."

At the time of this tragedy, Gustavo was a young man, barely eighteen years old. Although he had grown up in the church and participated in its activities, Gustavo had bigger dreams for life. Before graduation, Gustavo was recruited by Siemens, a German telecommunications company who took him under its wing as a young technician with a future in Germany. Gustavo was studying the German language and culture with dreams of professional studies in electronic engineering in Germany. Then his brother's brutal murder created a crisis in Gustavo's luke-

The Crocker family: Gustavo, Beth, Rachel, and Raquel

warm spirituality. He knew it was time to risk all in an intense search for Jesus, the Christ.

It was while earning his master's degree in Community Planning at the University of Cincinnati that Gustavo's total surrender to God's will came. This complete willingness to follow God helped him walk away from his job as a college professor in Guatemala after only a few weeks. "I had been teaching for only a month when we were asked to move to Quito, Ecuador, to serve as the South America Regional NCM Coordinator for the Church of the Nazarene. I told them I needed to check with my wife, Rachel. Her answer was immediate and emphatic: 'If God is calling us, let's go.' We have not looked back since."

About a year later, Gustavo was training leaders for NCM in Amman, Jordan, when God affirmed His calling to leave everything behind to follow Him. "While I was praying at Mount Nebo it became clear to me that the Promised Land was not across the Jordan River, but in the things of above. My pursuit for a religious Promised Land was over, and I surrendered my profession, career, future, and even ministry in exchange for the pursuit of God himself."

Sometimes that pursuit does not make sense at the time. Gustavo had received his theological training as a layman who was interested in deepening his walk with the Lord, yet later became ordained. He was an architect only by trade, yet he used his architectural skills for W & W projects. It was his study of the role of Christian charities in bringing about social transformation that became the bridge between his secular training and his further call to ministry.

This bridge led him to work as the denominational director of NCM International. Later he worked as field manager of Compassion International and then as senior vice president of ministry programs for World Relief. While the latter two ministry assignments could be seen as detours, in reality they provided excellent preparation for Dr. Crocker's current role as regional director for the Eurasia Region. He was exposed to some of the most qualified strategic minds working for the evangelical movement worldwide. His experiences taught him to integrate strategy, vision, and faith while working with global resources, indigenous leaders, and multicultural teams. In the process, he was also able to finish his PhD in Organizational Leadership from Regent University.

Perhaps the biggest challenge in becoming Regional Director was moving from pan-evangelical ministries that focused on organizational quality, program delivery, and accountability to a family-type ministry. We are harvesting decades of missionary work. Through these years of work, the Church has been able to instill in thousands of churches a solid faith in Christ, a solid doctrine of holiness, and a solid missional identity. At the same time, we have allowed ministry practices and traditions that were not necessarily part of the ethos of the Nazarene denomination but part of the missionaries' "practices back home" to become part of the church in the region.

One of these practices included—sometimes necessarily so—full trust but little accountability. Because I have been in ministries where financial and leadership accountability is of utmost importance, trying to apply these practices has been a challenge, especially when it has not been a practice in the past.

On the flip side of that, and having viewed up-close the leaders and programs from dozens of evangelical denominations, I can confidently say that there is something special and unique about the Nazarene family. It has given me the space to fulfill God's calling and vision for my life. Even though I have been formally trained in the areas of strategy, planning, and Christian leadership, it is the Nazarene Church that has been the best and most effective platform from which I have learned and developed as a leader.

Gustavo is the first to admit he is a beneficiary of the encouragement and leadership of several individuals. His local pastor, Rev. Leonel de Leon, gave him the opportunity to serve as a lay minister in his congregation. It was also under his leadership that Gustavo first began facilitating W & W projects in Guatemala. Later, he served the Mexico and Central America (MAC) Region as a volunteer architect on W & W projects with the encouragement of missionary Rev. Stanley Storey. These endeavors led to meeting Dr. Jerry Porter, then Regional Director for the MAC Region and supporter of the first non-U.S. W & W team, of which Gustavo was a leading member. Along with Dr. Steve Weber, the first NCM International Director, these leaders were instrumental in discovering, training, equipping, and enabling

Gustavo for global leadership within the Church and for the evangelical world at large.

It has not always been an easy road. Technically, nineteen years ago when the Crockers left Guatemala to serve in Ecuador, they were missionaries. However, the "system" at that time had not been fully developed to recognize global missionaries from the ends of the earth. One thing that has been helpful to them throughout their ministry is that their Guatemalan relational orientation has allowed them to feel at home in other cultures that also value community, family, and close relationships. This emphasis on relationships has been particularly helpful as a regional director who is responsible for more than one hundred missionaries and volunteers serving thirty-eight districts in thirty-four nations. Since they work with more than three thousand congregations, relationship building is critical.

Language also plays a key role in those relationships since the region has more than thirty official languages. It took twenty-three years, but in 2004 Gustavo finally discovered why God had him learn some German language and culture as a teenage boy in Guatemala: as the Eurasia Regional Director, his family now lives in Germany! Gustavo is also fluent in Spanish, English, Portuguese, and is studying Arabic.

Gustavo recognizes that he was blessed to follow in the footsteps of one of our denomination's finest missiologists, Dr. Franklin Cook, who built a strong and unified sense of mission and purpose on the region. Since 2004, the Lord has allowed the region to build on Dr. Cook's foundation through inspiration, challenge, and strategy that has blossomed into an amazing harvest. From 2004 to 2009, the region experienced an amazing 115 percent growth in membership that doubled the number of organized churches.

The biggest challenge we face is to deal with the various expectations that people have developed as a result of their own church culture. While the message of Christ is the same, some of the "Christian traditions" of each culture are often superimposed on other cultures, and this can cause clashes.

One exciting opportunity we have is the uniqueness of having some of our oldest churches (India, Britain) next door to some of our newest works (South Asia, Eastern Europe). This exchange allows us to inject new energy into some of our ministries that need renewal, while instilling experience in new works that need ecclesiological models. My daily prayer is that the Lord will give us wisdom and allow us to administer grace while facing the cultural realities of this vast region.

One cultural reality that Gustavo faces is the fact that his features are not distinctive to one people group. In the Middle East, people think he is from Egypt. In South Asia, people think he is Nepalese. In Europe, people think he is from Spain or Portugal. Sometimes this is funny, but it can also be risky, such as when he was mistaken as a Pakistani in India. On the other hand, Gustavo has been able to connect and travel with ease in many of the countries and cultures where Western missionaries may be viewed with suspicion.

Wherever he is, Gustavo always tries to be "culturally appropriate." When he was invited to preach at the largest church in Africa (Maputo, Mozambique), he decided to wear a beautiful African outfit that he had been given in West Africa. That Sunday he was so happy with his "African" look! As the pastor introduced him, he stated, "We have a guest speaker today. Please forgive Dr. Crocker's attire but that is the way they dress in his country." Much to his chagrin, Gustavo learned later that day that in the seventy-five year history of the church, he was the first male preacher without a suit and tie!

In the midst of all the cultural challenges, God's Spirit is moving, and Gustavo and Rachel are thankful to be a part of it. They support the Eurasia Region's vision to "Transform the world, in Christ, like Christ, for Christ." Their prayer is for a unity of identity and an integration of all ministries across the region. On a worldwide level, it is their prayer that the denomination will continue to develop the mindset that the Church is truly a global entity. They also hope that every world area of the Church will engage in supporting the global missionary work, and that the Church will be able to develop creative mechanisms to mobilize those called at the present time.

One way that Eurasia is encouraging this is by intentionally trying to have an equal number of volunteers and contracted missionaries. They also designed, promoted, and implemented the Isaiah and Caleb projects, which mobilized volunteers from Latin America into counties of similar culture and heritage such as the Middle East, Italy, Spain, and Portugal.

Through all of this, Gustavo is driven by the idea that God did not consider His deity something to be grasped, but took the form of a man—a poor man, a servant—to the point of death in the most offensive way known to man at the time: the cross.

"It is my privilege and duty to tell this amazing news to as many people as I can, using all the means that I can. Truly, the mission never ends! I am so blessed to be part of a Church that believes in His commands and commission—to be able to minister in a Church that is intentionally Christian, holiness, and missional. I pray that we will always continue our commitment to the last, the least, and the lost."

Message to the global Church: It is His Church. We must be responsible stewards of the doctrine and the core values that our denomination espouses—with no compromises whatsoever. On the other hand, we must understand that the richness of the Nazarene global family resides in our great variety of cultures, expressions, and languages.

8
No End in Sight

Rev. Jonas Mulate worked as a train engineer for thirteen years, but it was his passion for the "soul train" that has characterized his ministry of thirty-eight years. He and his wife, Lousada, have such a gift for evangelism that to list all the souls won and churches planted under their ministry would take up this entire chapter. Jonas gives the glory to God and credits a lot if it with the training he received as a child.

I am the product of Nazarene missions. I am also blessed to have grown up in a Christian family. My grandpa, Samuel Mulate, was an evangelist. My father, Rev. Lot Mulate, was a Nazarene pastor and district superintendent. I surrendered my life to the Lord at age thirteen when Nazarene missionary Mary Cooper shared the gospel with me and others under a tree. Two other missionaries, Lorraine Schultz and Rev. Stockwell, guided my growth as a Christian. Even the girl who stole my heart, Lousada Muchave, was the daughter of a Nazarene district superintendent.

How thankful I am for Nazarene global evangelism that produces a family worldwide!

Jonas and Lousada were married in 1971. At the time, Jonas was working as secretary to Dr. Floyd J. Perkins and also attending the Nazarene Seminary in Lourenco Marques (now Maputo). The next year, at age twenty-two, Jonas began his pastoral ministry at the Macian Church of the Nazarene in the Maputo District. A year later he served a mandatory year in the military. For the next thirteen years he served as a bi-vocational pastor of three churches, helping to grow the Maputo Church, now the largest Nazarene church in Africa. At that point, sensing the Lord's calling on his life, Rev. Mulate walked away from his well-paid job with the railroad to begin a new adventure with God.

> After I quit my job, it was like my vision broadened and I started living new challenges in the Lord's service. While still pastoring at Maputo, I went north to research what could be done to establish evangelical Nazarene churches in the midst of Catholic, Mormon, and Islamic strongholds. Along with 170 students, we traveled to these places, shared the gospel, and eventually established new churches across the region. Dr. Filimao Chambo and Dr. Dave Restrick were key supporters and collaborators in this church growth. Praise God!

Jonas and Lousada Mulate

In 1987, Jonas was offered a scholarship from the British Council and World Council of Churches to study English and Church Development at Oak Hill and Kingsmead Colleges in England. While he was studying there, Rev. Mulate was asked to preach in Nazarene churches across the country. In 1989, the year the Berlin Wall fell, Jonas was invited to East Germany to preach and to give counsel to Mozambicans and Angolans who were guest workers in the country.

Once back in Mozambique, the Mulates opened the work of the Church of the Nazarene in six provinces. From 1994 to 1996, Rev. Mulate served as district superintendent of both the North and Central Districts of Mozambique, at which time he was appointed as Catalytic Church Planter for Mozambique. His assignment was to open the work in the Inhambra Province, the last of ten Mozambican Provinces to be entered by the Church of the Nazarene. After just two years, the area was divided into two districts.

During a missions conference in Siteki, Swaziland, Jonas received his missionary calling as Dr. Nina Gunter spoke. After fifteen years of establishing churches in Mozambique, Jonas sensed God was calling him to share the gospel with people who didn't speak his language. Specifically, God was asking him to go to Angola. After an entire night of prayer, during which Jonas says he "felt like Jacob wrestling with the angel," Jonas told the Lord he would go if the denomination needed him.

> One thing that has amazed me with all of our moving around is how much God has blessed us with our children. We have five: three girls, Celina, Nelly, and Thelma; and two boys, Lot and Jonas Jr. They accompanied us in our ministry as we trekked all over northern Mozambique, then into Angola and later Botswana. In spite of the challenges we faced over the years, all of our children love God and support the work of the Church through their tithes and ministries at their local churches. They are graduates of Africa Nazarene University [ANU], for which

I will always thank Dr. Ted Esselstyn. His vision and compassion helped my children to attend. Though they are scattered across the globe now—Lot is an economist in Australia; Celina in Mozambique; Thelma is a lawyer; Nelly, whose husband is children's ministries coordinator for the Africa Region, is a business manager in South Africa; and Jonas is our most recent graduate from ANU in Kenya—we are united by our love for the Lord. Praise God, He is faithful!

God's faithfulness continued in the lives of the Mulate family as they stepped off the plane in their new home: Angola. Two months later, the Mulates officially opened the work through the launching of eight Nazarene churches in the Luanda area. On October 27, 2000, the Church of the Nazarene was officially recognized by the Angolan government.

In order to establish the church in Angola, we worked through evangelism. We would share the gospel, and people would become saved. Then they would bring their families, neighbors, and friends—just like Andrew brought Simon in the Bible. I also rode trains throughout Angola and distributed brochures that spoke about the church and how to accept Jesus and the Holy Spirit. The brochures had our personal contact information. We had lots of positive responses. We were asked to establish churches in differ-

Jonas (r.) with converts in Angola

ent areas and then we worked with helping a lay pastor take over. The next step was to help them receive theological training.

After two years, there were ten churches in Angola and five lay pastors had been sent to the seminary in Mozambique to study. After they graduated, they returned to Angola to help grow the ministry. The Mulates moved to the south of the country to plant more churches. All in all, from 2000 to 2007, the Mulates planted and organized churches in three Angolan provinces. During just seven years, the ministry grew into five districts with 76 churches and 6,900 full members, with 60 pastors, 10 district-licensed pastors, and 3 ordained elders. Today there are over 11,000 members and 89 pastors in Angola, with no end in sight!

In 2007 the Mulates were asked to minister in Botswana. The Church of the Nazarene had been there for thirty years, but for some reason growth had stalled at around three hundred people and fewer than ten churches. The Mulate's promise from God for their ministry in Botswana was, "I chose you and appointed you to go and bear fruit" (John 15:16). During their two short years there, the Mulates planted four churches, some in the Kalahari Desert area, and membership doubled to more than six hundred. They helped empower Botswana to have a national district superintendent for the very first time.

Even though the Mulates "retired" in 2009, their tireless efforts have no end in sight. Rev. Mulate is now serving as a commissioned evangelist in Mozambique. They have started a new ministry called African Eagle, which goes to minister at churches that the Mulates planted in their earlier years. Their vision is to empower Christians for ministry and to encourage and train new leaders.

Now, hop aboard, and use your own vision to imagine this: you are standing in immense, open grasslands. Through the middle runs a railroad track. As far as your eyes can see, the track continues on and on through the vast golden savannah. So it is with the "Mulate soul train!"

Message to the global Church: We fully enjoy the work of God. Please pray for us as we continue to promote the gospel in Mozambique. Truly we are together in this mission of evangelizing the world!

Epilogue
Endless

Harmon Schmelzenbach, an orphan from the U.S., was called by God to trek into the tiny kingdom of Swaziland to begin the work of the Church of the Nazarene. His church in Endzingeni was burned to the ground twice. Villagers hid when he came, so he stood in the middle of the huts and preached loudly so the locals could hear the message of salvation. It took more than two years, but finally his first convert was saved.

That same year in Swaziland, Salome Khumalo was born. Twelve years later, she visited Schmelzenbach's little church in Endzingeni and became saved. Her father, desiring the lobola (bride price) of cattle, engaged her to a non-Christian man. She refused to marry him and ran away several times to the church. Each time she was brought back and brutally whipped, but she refused to give up worshiping God. Her parents had her arrested and put in prison. Upon release, she fled to the church. She was then sent to the King's court for seven months of punishment. She prayed every day for God to protect her and save her. When the tribal authorities finally sent her home, she ran away again to the mission. Finally, her parents gave up on her.

Salome had a passion to reach the lost. In 1950 she became a missionary from Swaziland to South Africa, beginning the first urban Nazarene church in what is now known as Soweto in the Johannesburg area. During a tent revival in the early work there, a brash young man entered with his friends, intent on disrupting the services. Instead, young Andrew Matshedisho became saved. He began prayer meetings in his home and later went on to train at the Nazarene Bible College. Twelve preachers came out of Andrew's ministry. One of these was July Ndlovu. He went to Zimbabwe and helped begin the work of the Church of the Nazarene there, later becoming a district superintendent.

When Rev. Ndlovu was preaching during a revival service in Zimbabwe, a young seven-year-old boy gave his life to Christ. His name was Cosmos Mutowa—who went on to become ordained, taught at the Nazarene Bible College in Harare, and was a leading pastor in Zimbabwe. He and his wife served as missionaries in The Republic of Malawi and were commissioned as Global Missionaries. Today Rev. Cosmos Mutowa is serving as a leader for the entire Africa Region as the NCM Coordinator, ministering in thirty-six countries and impacting countless lives.

God's amazing work of salvation through the witness of obedient missionaries, pastors, and laypeople is endless. It goes on around the globe as the Holy Spirit continues His work of prevenient grace, wooing a lost world to himself. Only in heaven will we truly understand and see how God has forged every testimony, every new birth, every miracle of grace into His Kingdom—from the ends of the earth.

A Call to Action: The Ending Is Up To You

- Fast and pray for individuals around the world who are called to missionary service to have the courage to say yes to God.
- Add missionaries from other countries to your prayer list. Pray for them to have wisdom and strength.
- Actively seek to have missionaries from other cultures come to speak at your church. Don't worry about possible language barriers. Smiles and hugs and offers to pray go a long way!
- Encourage children in your church to become pen pals with missionary kids from other cultures.
- Pray for our missionary training centers around the world, for funding and labor to be provided so that God-called individuals may receive the training they need to be effective missionaries of the gospel.
- Pray for all missionaries to have peace about their children's futures.
- Educate your church about the scope of missionaries called from around the globe.
- Ask God for worldwide revival.

Notes

1. Charles R. Gailey and Howard Culbertson, *Discovering Missions*, (Kansas City: Beacon Hill Press of Kansas City, 2007).

2. Dr. Louie E. Bustle, "2009 Global Mission Report."

3. Marvin Olasky, "Fear God, Work Hard," *WORLD*, November 10, 2007.

4. Prior to regular status, a district has not yet become self-sustaining; it does not yet have all the rights and privileges of a district, such as sending voting members to General Assembly.

5. Creative access countries are those that do not allow persons who are openly missionaries. To gain entrance, they must have another occupation, such as teaching, or medical training.

6. Alpha USA, "What is Alpha—Spiritually?" *The Alpha Course*, http://alphausa.org/Groups/1000052640/What_is_Alpha.aspx (accessed June 15, 2011).

Author's Bio

Rev. Ellen Gailey Decker is an ordained elder in the Church of the Nazarene. An MK (missionary kid) from Swaziland, Africa, Ellen has lived on three continents and traveled to almost thirty countries.

Ellen is the author of two books, *Africa's Soul Hope* and *The Power of One*. She is also the founding editor of *NCM Magazine*.

Her life verse is Acts 20:24, "I consider my life worth nothing to me, if only I may finish the race and complete the task the Lord Jesus has given me—the task of testifying to the gospel of God's grace."